W9-BTP-690

The Feral Love Poems

The Feral Love Poems

Joey Brown

Copyright © 2020 Joey Brown

All rights reserved. No part of this book may be reproduced, stored in a retreival system, or transmitted by any means, electronic, mechanical, photocopying, recording, or otherwise, without written permission from the author.

ISBN: 978-1-7350976-1-9
(Hungry Buzzard Press)

Published by:

Hungry Buzzard Press
P.O. Box 80164
Keller, TX 76248-2300

Contents

Peace Be With Us

you can't get there from here

Portraits

Feral Love

Now That We Know the Route We Are Taking

About the Author

For Howie

With gratitude to the following journals, which served as the original homes of these poems:

bordertown: Tattoo
Concho River Review: The Trees of North Texas
Cybersoleil: The Last Hill Before Oklahoma
The Oklahoma Review: Intersection of Crow and Dead Possum; The Cleaning House List; The Inside Outsider
The Dragon Poet Review: The Losing of Things
The Dos Passos Review: The Transitive Property
EDGE: a girl, maybe seventeen, comes out of the laundry
Langdon Review: A Journal of the Arts in Texas: Rita; Gary's Girl; Joe, My Neighbor Says; Denny Thinks About the Reasons for Leaving; If I Knew Where
Louisiana Review: Feral Love
The Mid-America Poetry Review: doing Ophelia's mad scene
The Red Earth Review: Peace Be With Us; The picture the way I remember it; The Widow Shows Me Around the House
The Sea Letter: The Fate of Some Minnows: Comanche Lake c. 1975
Tulsa Review: Different River, Different Rock

Peace Be With Us

In Texas, A Constant Sense of Motion

In Texas, a constant sense of motion
derives from the click-and-hum of
concrete-sectioned highways
and from rises so subtle
they can not be felt
until the elongated ribbon I follow
carries me down again.

I mean West Texas, of course,
west of here, then south,
where the curves are all muted
in their arcs.
Mesquite populates the pastures,
houses are sparse,
intersection serve as towns,
and I am lulled into long-term memory.

This is terrestrial motion,
unmapped and unnamed
in both science and romance.
The diurnal routine of travel,
of move, rest,
move rest
a cellular clemency
conferred by the landscape.

In Texas, when I lie down at night to sleep,
drift between the hynopompic and the hypnogogic,
those fields of mesquite pop phosphemic
in my periphery.
Kaleidoscopes of silt bank up on
fading sunlight.
My body rides,
wends toward the ether.

The Trees of North Texas

Wayfinding depends on an architecture,
whether vernacular or natural.
But on the road outside Throckmorton
the trees of North Texas
disguise their roles as your helpmates.

They reside in fields science calls
the topographical void,
confirming their measure
in the syntax of this place.

But what do you know of these trees?
You knew the big ones, once:
hollies and ash, alder and oak.
But can you choose the chinquapin
from the Monterrey now?

The burs you know,
their loose wide canopies
drench the asphalt in shadow.
And the live oaks,
the ones of impossibly long, old man arms
that slice the sunlight into Whitman's centrifugal spokes
just so briefly
a beam from some divine –ism
glances off you like a leaf.

You range, tree to tree,
oak to oak,
feel their weight as they anchor the sky,
hold it low
so that transient events
read out as clearly here
as in any telescope's viewfinder.

Astronomers would say no:
Not enough hills, too many trees.

Out here, bodies at rest stay at rest,
and bodies at rest grow old.

You will not know
one tree from the others.
But follow them.
Roll through the lack of axial space,
home
if you know how it feels.

Intersection of Crow and Dead Possum

On a highway east of Tulsa
rain and thunder bring an interstate's worth
of traffic to a stop. So I watch a crow eat
from the carcass of a dead possum.
Flicks a glance at me, chop-steps
his way between dinner and my tire.
I am not even a scandal in his day.
But he is a prize I find on the road
out writing my plains cartography.
Sometimes when I drive I say prayers
for people who need them.
Sometimes I add myself.

I wait on weather and traffic,
on some unnamable feeling,
opportunity to put the right words to it.
It's about there and getting there,
about spanning space and breadth,
a compilation of vowels
and wads of connotation,
perfect, if only I knew
how it is pronounced.

Between the Cherokee Casino
and the yard of rusting tractor parts
is the sign that says
today is a gift from God,
and I wonder what the rest have been.

Gears on a cement mixer shudder,
and the crow extends a protective wing.
The possum emanates rot and lies there
like a fact. Thunder when it is far off rattles
you inside, but this one hits us hard and crisp.
I ease off the brake.
Crow blinks.

Peace Be With Us

Things from your town of no use in the world:
the shortcut through the pecan groves to the river,
knowledge of Stephens County roads,
the radio soundtrack fit tight for driving,
skills at wayfinding—non-transferable by nature—
remembering to stick you hand
out the window and
feel undulations of summer
push against your palm.
No, even the wind elsewhere is not the same.

You have forfeited being prepared.
If we look now, there is no flashlight
rolling around your floorboards.
No loop of baling wire, pliers,
green Halliburton tape.
No just-in-case rations nor five-dollar bill
in the glove compartment.
Lost is nostalgia to you now,
paper maps only wall decoration,
and with the world the way it is is these days
we see why you think the way you do.

Among skills gained you might list these:
locating soft places to crash,
a healthy fear of lightning,
knowing when the song is worth staying until the end,
stillness borne of letting someone quit you,
understanding of the "Peace Be With Us"
graffiti on the water tower
by the school, the one they painted over,
that bled through, clear as day,
the entire time between
fourth grade and senior year,
the one no one said they got—
and you asked—but now?
But now.

Tattoo

As if a jar of red dirt
can hold
bones   skin   sight,
or ink a soul color
a permanent stain
that says who I am
and wears like glass.
Cartography
points west
carves and cuts
the plain's arc,
leaves me
looking out for words,
but what rides over
had already been said.
Spasms, like a name,
stamp into me
location on my skin.
The map breathes out,
pushing me
in all directions.

The Last Hill Before Oklahoma

*"In a word, the boundaries of the Ozarks are vague to most people
and subject to interpretation and disagreement by the experts."*
Milton Rafferty, The Ozarks as a Region: A Geographer's
Description

At first
I felt the border like a paper cut
that nagged all the time for my attention

So I learned
a dozen places
I could drive to in minutes
to get to the border
see the border
invisible
itching

You ever hear a place call to you
the air or
the dirt

It was like that

Later I learned
the plains meet the hills
in a paradox
intercut and interwoven
no books
no border

As much like hill country as it looks
I am living
on the plains

I took the house
on the last hill before Oklahoma

an echo made by the Boston Mountains
in their creation
upland
in prairie grasses
same dirt
same air

If I Knew Where

I would tell you where to meet me
if I knew where.
Would that you might recognize
the land of early summer sunsets,
without the sentimentality.
The scent of burgeoning greens amid
blazes of pink and orange
that always seem,
in spite of their
night-after-night appearances,
impossible.

It's dust.
Just dust,
someone,
everyone,
is wont to tell me.
The remnants of incurable
twenty-first century drought
drifting over Oklahoma.
It's not what sunset looks like,
but says who.

There
I inhale Mother Nature's exhalations:
fruit blossoms and wheat grass
weeds amoking through the fields
that outskirt the gray and heat
of town.
Promise this much to me:
after supper
you'll turn west,
breathe in deep then deeper—
until you taste the red clay—
until the magnetic hum
trembles in your fingertips.

Listening

The wind gives each tree its own tone

low, rising, building melodic, harmonic
traveling across the tops of trees
the rustling, rattling, clattering, smashing
of leaves

Wind
pushing the sunlight west
drying out the hide of the dog lying nearby
bringing early fall pears to the ground

you can't get there from here

Arriving in the Off-Season: Picher, Oklahoma 2005

The first thing I saw was a man
wearing a quilted parka and
riding a bike uphill.
It was August.
He was the only living thing I found.

Brown water puddled
without rain or working plumbing,
skeletonized houses
without doors or windows,
ghosts of trees
without leaves or bark,
miles of highway
without cars.

I admit I wanted to see
what was left,
whatever had fallen out of their pockets
and aligned the ditches,
to mark the distance between there
and my good night's sleep.

In my driveway
I beat the dust from my clothes,
fearful of the grains of chat
that rode back with me
when I made flight.

U.S. Geological Survey

The ground here shifts
when no one is watching
Tumbling, spilling,
cracking felt in the soft
clicks of electronics
jars in the cabinets
rearranging by millimeters
We never let on how near
resides disaster

We've put faith in
what came before us
clay and shale and
layers built over time
We invented math and
fragile shelters but we've
willfully, quietly, disregarded
the history of all surveying
and dirt being
what it is

The earth will first
take down the bones
A thousand years from now
it will roil them back up
and yet we draw lines and curves
as if to say what nature is
all of it traceable
even us

Explaining Here to My Mother-in-Law

My mother-in-law heads to the pool,
the early May water too cool
for the rest of us,
when I warn her
to watch out for the stickers.

Stickers? she asks.
What in God's hell are stickers?

For a second images of all of them,
goatheads to sand burs,
run through my mind,
and I realize I have no way
to explain stickers to someone
who has never seen one.
That she is the first person
I have known
who has never had to balance on one foot
while extracting an offender
from the other.

We have already covered
chiggers,
yellow jackets,
fiddlebacks,
deer tick fever,
the paths tornadoes prefer,
why the sky is red sometimes,
that the sirens she hears at dawn
are really just coyotes,
and whether cows are mean.
I have done little to assuage her fears:
I am the reason her only son
lives in the constant presence of death.

But at night,
from our perch overhanging the
beginning of the Ozarks,
we watch fingers of the longest, slowest sunset
you could ever hope to see,
and listen
to the quietest night
she has ever not heard.

The First Thing I Notice in Corpus

Grime. They'll get me for that, but grime
is the first thing I notice. No,

refineries are the first thing.
The smell. I am familiar,
from having grown up in the Oklahoma
where a refinery looms across the road
from our elementary school.
The smell does not sicken me
the way I imagine it might first-timers.
But the refineries:
so many of them. They dot fields,
like farmhouses—farmhouses
that give off roiling toxic smoke
beyond expanses of grass
weirdly green in winter.

And not the hotel, which is fine,
or fine enough. Seven minutes from the beach
comes with a view of the highway, the abandoned
Mexican restaurant across the street,
a long row of dumpsters, palm trees thicker
than I had dreamed they could ever be
and that somehow appear wilted.

They're renovating the floor above
mine. My window overlooks the alley,
where I watch a construction worker
on his phone. He leans over the hood,
pulls his hair, paces the length of the truck.
When he hangs up, he sits in the driver's seat,
door still open, left foot on the ground as if to run.
He's draped over the steering wheel.
I think he's crying.

Concrete poured onto the beach makes stairs
and benches, stems erosion determined to do its job.
I left work for this, feel my stealth
was not worth it. Behind me a cliff-high
row of mansions sits weathered,
their Mediterranean facades incongruous
to this part of Texas,
and to my expectations.
All are under off-season repair.
Plastic bottles bob at my feet.
A Cheetos bag tags the concrete slope, spins
like a star, tags again. The people sitting
in their cars must be locals.
as I am the only one not to know
seagulls take aim like bullets.

Three nights I lie in bed and listen
to the thick traffic, don't feel sorry for myself.
There is no place in Corpus,
no time without
the racket: horns and jake brakes,
music and talk radio thumping
out of every second car,
cursing in three languages,
gulf winds that whip you down.

Different River, Different Rock

I step into water running southerly, easterly,water that, were
I not so stubborn, would carry me from home.
I walk against a current that turns me, turns me,
and I am half a mile from camp before I think of directions again.
I am here because I went on the road, on a tear,
the way I go for state lines and highways,
historical markers as if they mean something.
This time I drove with one arm out the window,
wind sharp enough to cut skin.

A black catfish walks the water with me.
His size suggests he is old, and the way he weaves ahead of me,
then drifts back to me when the basin makes my going slow,
shows his comfort with travelers in his river.
I stop to watch him, and he stops, too.
His whiskers sting my legs.
I imagine he lingers in thoughts of waywardness,
but really it is the warm stirring of the water he misses.
I reach down to touch his head.

Before my fingers break the surface, he is gone.
I come up with a wafer of black shale,
a hundred years of puréed sand pressed into its layers.
Two fathers and two sons unload gear and a yellow dog,
push their canoes into my stream of consciousness.
I finger the broken tip of the shale, its one rough edge,
and wonder how long I have stood thinking about all I do
not hold.

The Transitive Property

She accepted as fact the edge of the world
lay five miles outside of town.
Maybe it was eight, could've been ten,
particulars didn't so much matter.
From the bed of a pickup,
the fastest real estate going,
she saw all she cared to see.
Living full of sugar,
she paid attention to how she walked,
thought her name was fine for saying anything.
She hovered between sensation and knowing,
off with those boys again.
If someone played a song on the radio for you
that meant something real, didn't it?
She lost count of her lies nearly every day.
If she'd caught inertia back then,
saved all the juice and the sweetness of breath,
couldn't you call her fortune,
girl of the sojourning spirit,
to be ravished before she knew the word.

Wish for someone to let her down easy,
for the cold to slide off her skin, to forget
all madness comes from lovesickness.
She's not sorry, at least not the way you want her to be,
and she's not asking your forgiveness.
Pluck the petals
and the juice squeezes out,
residue never as fine as the name.
After a while grace just is, even if the definition
arrives unexpected. And as long as we're wishing,
would you spin down the time,
would you tell that girl in the pickup
where this is headed.
Say: sometimes you just hold on
until you get something going

and you likely won't remember how.
Say: I wonder, sugar,
are you still there? But in the world this big,
how could you be.

The Losing of Things

Keys,
the wallet,
then the money in it,
the bag someone gave her for bringing here to work.
Only when you watch her
rummage among the piles on her desk,
lift up the folders to view the empty spaces beneath,
feel for the contents of pockets that aren't there
do you realize that is not her dress.
At least it wasn't until this week, when she came to be
wearing the lines of the storm
and hand-me-down clothes.

After the house
it came every little thing went missing,
though whether by natural motion
or its own accord she could never tell.
Even time, she says, looking around her office,
as if glancing over bookshelves can give dimensions
to her sense she's supposed to be somewhere just now.
Where, though, is an answer carried up with the draft,
with bits and whits she'd once had a lot of,
lost or mixed into strange context so that even as she looks
right at them she does not see them.

It's all in the rubble,
she tells you, somewhere,
the gesture she makes with her arm
not meant to point your attention at any specific pile
so much as it is meant to sweep the image of her own
hubbled home off her mind.
You don't know if you should laugh,
even though she does,
at her sudden onset of absentmindedness,
the abrupt fluidity of time,
at the way the losing of things takes more than a day.

you can't get there from here

but you can ride eye-level to tall grasses
crowding barbed wire, where the seeds float
upwards with dust motes,
where port sand coats your skin.

You can idle at a red light, where girls sit
talking lies in the car one lane over,
where a man, wallet in hand,
runs from the Sac and Fox casino,
where the last of those listening
to the radio have the volume up
You can land in the parking lot
of what used to be a restaurant,
where grease hangs in the humidity,
where dead arguments cling
to vibrations made by trees.

You can't get there from here
but you can find the place they're living
in the absence of bees,
where caterpillars eat the slow
and steady growth, where geese maunder
trapped between seasons.
You can get back to where your grade school
became a haunted house, became a café,
became the bingo parlor,
became nothing but a set a steps
once it burned down.

You can't get there from here
but you can get far enough away to be a rumor,
to where the story falls apart,
to where coming back is too far gone.

all the places you will ever live

A woman who wants
to call me sister
tells me to buy a house.
She knows the one:
a house in a little town
ten miles from here,
a little house
between rocks and dogwoods,
a little house that lives here.
But she is not from here
anymore than I.

And shouldn't you trust
locals only when learning
the lay of the land.
Her ten miles is only
halfway there.
Off by a fraction of an inch
multiples into miles
the farther I drive.

A man who's lived
here longer than I've breathed
tells me winters carry
in little snow. Fails
to say that when the snow
comes, it smothers
all effort, bustle, and deed.

Houses built along bluffs,
roads driven into valleys.
The rises and falls
of this place
speak together,
but not
to each other.

The sky here tells me
all architectures
are paper boundaries,
that everything built
will leave the earth,
that grief
fills all the places
you will ever live,
that edges
call you
to fall away.

The Widow Shows Me Around the House

Spring 1991: the widow calls me.
Not quite two weeks since
her husband's funeral.
Will I take her to the movies.
She is not particular
what we see or where we go.
Just needs out of that house.
Up the country road pitted with mudholes,
up to the derelict artifact of a rich
territory farmer's life.
Glass panes rattle in the front door that drags
as she opens it. Eight years left on a fifteen-year
mortgage, she tells me right away.
Had he divorced her instead,
she would kill him just for that.

Rooms open onto rooms, each crammed
with garage sale furniture curated
in attempt at the period.
Dust, chintz, threadbare rugs in the parlor,
an honest to god parlor.
People will bring you too much ham
when your husband dies, she says.
And the freezer on the fritz. She shrugs.
On the rolled arm of the velvet sofa
lies a packet just back from Kodak.
Of the funeral. Doc, she calls him,
in his casket. If I want to see.
It's okay that I don't, she says.
Most people don't.

We parade through each room in turn.
Do I see. Isn't it something.
She narrates their histories
of meals prepared and eaten,
sleeping rituals of the moved-away children,

how it came about she has lived in the big bedroom
alone for some months now.
Grime, floorboards missing,
pre-war plumbing fixtures
in a mold-smelling bathroom,
peeling wallpaper behind a bunk bed, unmade.

Something over the garage she wants
to show me. Opens the door onto
a little apartment fitting neither now nor then.
Nubby blue couch, 7-11 cups and mail collected on
a kidney-shaped coffee table. Brand new elliptical
just inside the door, the mass of cardboard once
encasing it leaned on a wall.
He had lived up here a while, she says.
And, of course, this is where he died.
Does not point. But I think I see
the shape amid the coupons and circulars
from the paper of two Sundays ago
lying on the floor.

He never did do anything to help himself,
she says. The door clicks, she turns
the key, and by testing the lock is locked,
ends our tour of the house.
We head for town, no idea the time
of the matinee. She wears page seventeen
of the Spiegel summer catalog. Haircut since
the funeral. Another husband will materialize
at some point, she says. Lays fingertips to the
flying-by landscape beyond her window.
You just have to be willing to take things as-is.
Do I want to know how she'll kill the albatross.
A for sale sign at the end of the road. She will paint it
herself. Highest bidder takes all. Land, furniture,
linens, every dented fork in the stormy,
junk-drunk house.

The Inside Outsider

At the Hop and Sack
the grandmother working the register
tells me she likes my top,
points with her hand full of my change.
This is just before I remind her
we went to high school together
and she comes around the counter to give me a hug,
longer and harder than what we both really feel.

This is the place where
they're playing church league softball
like it's the meaning of life,
where the festival of a minor god,
a state politician or a basketball player,
happens this Saturday,
where tables of homemade crafts accompany
$5 plates of fire department BBQ you can eat
at the picnic tables crowding blocked-off streets.

This is the place where
once upon a time my mettle was measured
by how far back into Fairlawn Cemetery
I could make it from the road,
where I was denied a badge
because from the road to the back
of Tucker Cemetery was
never going to happen.

This is the place where
I am gifted reminiscences
of people I don't know
and don't remember
with "You know her. Jamie's sister's kid?"
And I say, for the umpteenth time,
no.
I never knew Jamie,

who was five grades ahead of me,
and never met her sister,
who was grades ahead still,
and I would not know any of their kids
were they to plough into me now
where I stand on the street,
lost under the eaves of Grundy's Drug.

This is the place where
my not returning after college
to get a decent job,
and to obsess about babies,
and my babies' babies,
makes me a special kind of outsider,
an inside-outsider,
who knows them
and is known by them
but who doesn't
and who isn't.

Portraits

Rita

I don't know what Rita knows,
only that I talk to her when I am in the grocery store.
She remembers what she asked you
and what you said the last time you were in.
Passes out Kleenex if you need one,
pushes carts for old people,
or, rather, very old people,
seeing how she is already my mother's age.
But then she does have that mother feeling,
which is why I flutter up to her as I always have
to women who feel to me like mothers.

I don't know what Rita knows,
but I listen when she talks.
When she's on smoke break on the bench out front
I hear her call the bread man "hon."
She says "hon" like you say "Oklahoma,"
and the way she says it
reminds me how many small things here
are different from there.
She says "hon" like you say "home,"
so sometimes I think about asking Rita
where she's from,
but I don't want to be told
she's not who I think she is.

Betty

Betty checks my groceries at Summer Fresh
since leaving her job at the liquor store next door.
She likes to tell me old wives' tales,
but then she is an old wife,
and then I am open to such woman-words.

She tells me the names of grandbabies and daughters,
says the places they all used to be from.
We talk like old friends,
or at least good acquaintances,
and I am alright that she doesn't know my name.

Betty tells me the weather, warns me what's to come,
instructs me to cleave open persimmons
if I want to know what winter will bring.
She draws, her finger on my palm,
the shapes I am to look for,
which one means ice and which one calm.
It is excellent advice,
if I don't forget it, now.

Adam: Imagined and Past Tense

Adam of the blue pickup
going the speed limit
and no more
highway skirting Fort Worth
one of the mean parts
far enough out
reminds you this is just Texas

Quiet
likes waiting
does mostly as he's told
knows the world
bigger than he is

If his desire is to move
someone moves him
puts him where
they think he goes

He doesn't always appreciate
the resulting perspective
aware he sees
the funny angles

Adam of the blue pickup
white t-shirt
baseball player haircut
wrist resting on steering wheel
window down
music of reasonable volume

Eyeline and horizon
all bigger than he keeps track of

Sometimes he wakes up
senses he's just been moving
air sweeping past his arms
Somewhere he is fast
moves when he wants

Jewel

I see Jewel.
But not Jewel when I knew her.
This is Jewel that night in the airport,
spinning in the arms of a dark-haired
younger man, spinning like only someone
who has been missing love can.
Jewel in her Capri pants,
worn in any season,
her dainty slides and whorled hair.
Jewel, both thin and round,
with the heavy wild grace
of a tango dancer, and a string of muscle
in her upper arm. Jewel, the intricacies
of whose movements make me jealous to my core.Jewel,
twenty years older than me,
still so much farther beyond me. She laughs
like someone holding a glass of wine
out on the patio, on a night in June,
at a party too fancy to have been given
for no reason. She covers her face with her hands,
smile sluicing around her fingers.
She claims she is embarrassed,
but she has said what she thinks.
Maybe she cries when she says it,
but she gets it all out,
and by the time she falls asleep,
I am sure she is clean.

Waitress

On dollar Corona night we learn a lot in eight minutes:

that Tuesday is always a small crowd,
she used to work that one skanky bar in Carthage,
she'd get the chicken nachos if we were her,
that her name is Mary Ellen
but we can call her Mickey because,
you know,
we're cool.

We are her only table so far because,
you know,
her boss is a dick.
She wears black from hair to nails,
lipstick so purple it could be,
smiles more than you would expect,
leans hard on our table when she talks,
giggles like water flowing out of a faucet.

Her husband is the bartender,
she thinks old drunks are the saddest,
had a tracheotomy once but thoughtfully spares us why.
She's waiting,
she says,
for a new place to open up,
something fancy this town has never seen.
She and hubby can run it together.
You know,
classy,
she says walking away,
our empties bashing and clanking in her arms.

Gary's Girl

You can't name a thing
she doesn't feel,
Gary's girl, that is,
from the soles of her feet on up.
Love and fighting,
anger and crying,
it takes hold of her cells.
All of her cells,
streaming in her blood,
so that she's living out her convictions,
molting, one self into another,
living in her light.

Can you see it,
looking at her now:
gray haired and sun-worn.
A faded woman in girls' clothes.
She's holding a carton of cigarettes
at the intersection of 20th and Main,
waiting on the light to change,
talking to a boy.

Gary, from what we know,
may've been alright.
The kind to lean in straight lines,
we can guess,
because how bad can a guy be
if his girl wears his name
scripted on her neck:
right side
blue ink
and curlicued?

Maybe he was a good,
but she couldn't tell you now.

She lit out,
from here and
from him.
Got sixteen different stories of where.

You think you've caught her in the nowhere,
a low place,
her falling place.
But, honey, you can't dream
the worst she has seen.

Feelings, she'll tell you,
are burning at her heels.
So she's moving,
she's always moving.
What matter that it's the track
between the Easy Mart and Hollow Hill.
You won't catch grass growing
under her feet.
You will not catch her at all.

Stephanie, Pt. 1

I wake up to a radio, from the neighbor's house
I think, playing a long garbling string of
notes and words I cannot understand. It is deep in
the night after a long February day of no comfort,
and I want to forgive all for a little sleep when the notes
pitch up like a scream. Somebody is screaming.
And before I can stumble my way to the living room window
somebody is begging. It's that boy Stephanie is
married to. He's hanging over the fence like an abandoned
dog, while Stephanie stands in the road halfway between
their house and mine, her hands covering her face.
Both of them are crying, wailing like sick animals, in that way
only the most grief stricken of people do but even then, only
when nobody else can hear them.

She takes one step backward and the boy hollers no,
snapping the wheels in her loose. So she takes off running.
But that boy's moaning drags on her like an anchor,
and she's done stopped by the end of the block. She throws
her head forward, puts her hands on her knees like a runner
exhausted by the distances both ahead of and behind her would.
The boy sinks to his knees, crying, both of them crying,
all of us breathing hard. She hesitates in every direction,
confusion buzzing around each of her movements. She waits
out both their tears and the noise in her head,
walks back into their yard, opens the chain link gate
and without looking at her own husband,
she goes into the house alone.

She picks her way through that little house,
light after light coming on as she moves, runs as any fool could tell.
Any fool, that is, but that boy she married, sitting in the front yard,
drowning in his own sadness, so maybe that's why he lets her go.
She's out in the road again, still running, and now she's got
that baby with her. Little things she scooped up with the baby
are dropping behind her, but this time she keeps running.

51

This time the old man next door is outside saying oh, honey.
This time I hear her heels click on the road and that boy
slam on the chain link fence. This time she runs past the stop sign
and the neighbors' porch lights, and the headlight beams of the
police car coming over the hill. Stephanie runs headlong
into the dark, that baby screaming to beat it all,
and it's hard to say who I am most afraid for.

Joe, My Neighbor Says

My neighbor knocks,
always a minute or two after eight a.m.
because before eight is unneighborly.
Today he's come to tell me
Joe is dead.

Joe, who I knew only to wave at,
Joe, whose work required flatbed trailers of lumber,
Joe, who laughed "I'll be damned,"
Joe, who was fifty-six, my neighbor says:
Joe is dead.

My neighbor hands me a grocery bag
of his homegrown tomatoes,
puts his hands in his pockets,
takes them out again.

Joe was working, stacking salvaged windows.
Joe was making floorboards new again.
Joe was going to make that house
look like a million bucks.
Joe's son was there.
Joe is dead.

My neighbor's eyes scan the street.
He rocks on his heels,
hands in pockets,
out of pockets.
I add small words, vague and insubstantial,
until my neighbor looks right at me
and I find his pain unspeakable.

These aren't as good as last year's,
he says. The tomatoes. He knows
how much I liked them last year.
Joe, coffee cup in hand as they talked in the driveway.

Joe, Coors Light can in hand as they talked in the driveway.
Good guy, my neighbor says.
Now Joe is dead.

My neighbor's hands pause
their travel between air and pockets,
touch palm to palm.
We both look at the scars and nicks
and crooks of his old man hands.
We both look at the supplicant arc gravity makes
with his limbs as he lets his hands fall.
We both look over at his driveway
then look away.

a girl, maybe seventeen, comes out of the laundry

a girl, maybe seventeen, comes out of the laundry
baby in a ratty diaper slung over one hip
baby's got no hair, no shoes, no clothes
just grape jelly on its face

she plunks the baby on the sidewalk
in grit blown up from the parking lot
plunks herself down, exhausted-like,
on a bench beneath the payphone

she crosses her legs, shows the blackened bottoms
of her bare feet, picks at her chipped nails,
squints into the sun, watches cars and birds
looks anywhere but the sidewalk

her T-shirt is threadbare, tight and pink
she's got her hair done up
black liner rings around her eyes
she will not stop touching her lips

after a while she gets up and
uses the payphone, seems to push
too many buttons, says loud "Co-llect.
What, you don't do that no more?"

few quiet words come before the
bitching and cussing, things like
"yeah, well, she better, she knows
I ain't gonna do none-a that shit"

she hangs up hard when a guy
in an old Camaro pulls into the lot,
swings the Bondoed door
just does miss the baby

she's got her hands on her hips already
waiting, but the guy just points
at the moving-away baby, too hot
for a baby outside, and then on the concrete

the girl gives the guy the finger
uses both hands, goes to stand in
the laundry door, leans into the
darkness like there's nobody there

Feral Love

Denny Thinks About the Reasons for Leaving

Because the husband sprang it on her—
on them—
while guests in his living room,
Denny thinks about the reasons for leaving.

Pinot noir resting in globes,
Ritz crumbs collecting on clothes,
the one-inch-by-one-inch squares of cheese
hardening at their corners, and the husband says
"I'm leaving.
Because."

Because
he feels there's more expectation than
momentum in the universe,
and the future he's afraid will never happen
sits lonely in the dark corners of his house.
Because, the husband says,
he wanted her to be with friends when he told her.

Because
by leaving we mean left:
after putting on the jacket he'd laid
ready over the stair railing
on arriving, then left
in his car to the airport in Kansas City,
left his wife.

And because the wife cries
in that air-gulping way of one
who's taken off guard by sudden grief,
and because his own wife runs to the kitchen
to snap off burners,
because embarrassment wells up in him
like nausea, Denny pretends
there's just-remembered work,
somehow more urgent than this,
waiting in another room.

Because he answers the phone
when the husband calls
                    "Because."
There's Helen, a woman from his office,
who loves him, he thinks, even though
she would not come with him.
                    "Because."
Denny says, "maybe you've overblown this whole thing."

Because,
the husband says,
he's got to catch a plane,
and then a plan,
somewhere in South America.
His favorite professor lives there still,
he thinks. That guy, in his nineties, now.
And the name of the town, and even the country,
the husband isn't sure of. But he'd always wished
he'd gone into archeology,
and if not now when.

Because
the husband's wife lies in the guest room
after taking two Valuim scrounged from a drawer,
because quiet in some houses rests so tenuously,
because one brief scene alters the definitions of so many
words;
                    just Because.
Denny keeps his wife talking as they lie in bed,
about this night
and these people
and anything he can think to bring up.
They hold hands over the covers, and
even as sleep overtakes her speech,
Denny still talks
                    Because
of what he thinks of in the dark.

The Cleaning House List

You start with

1. Clean House
because you can't write a note
saying

1. Get your life up off the floor.
Besides, the real problem is much more
cluttered than that:
just how does one clean house?

1. Sew loose, disembodied buttons on.
But sew on to what? Such a small, tedious job.
And really, do they look so bad collected
in jars here and there?

1. Match up socks. Easy enough.
So how do you end up off washing out pantyhose
in the grungy bathroom sink?

1. Sort taxes/insurance. Let the shuddering
ensue. Construct a hasty tower of babbling paperwork,
ignore all dates and the alphabet, as well.

1. Closets. Too boring.

1. Kitchen cabinets. More boring.
We're lacking motivation over here.

1. Chests of drawers. Ah, but what of the need
for places to tuck
found pennies, loose papers, and pens?

1. Love letters. But, no, not them.
They are so brittle and thin, tremble like ash in your hands.
Trap them under a lid that won't fit
its dented pot, along with
a sweetness you would rather not name.

1.

When details belong to both god and the devil,
order is, at best, only implied. You start off with

1. Clean House

because that is just how all lists start.

Unpacked on the Interstate

Between mile marker 326 on the Oklahoma side
and 11 on the Missouri side,
someone unpacked him:

the cluster of balled-together socks,
easy to miss in the ditch;

t-shirts folded into a neat stack
as if just lifted from the shelf in JC Penney;

assorted mall shopping bags recycled
into luggage, all about to spill;

three shoe boxes duct-taped into a convenient-to-move tower,
scuffed and dented by the tumble they took at speed;

one of those cardboard pop-up chests of drawers
they sell to college kids teetering on the median;

more socks, these loose, thrown,
so they draped on clumps of winter weeds;

then the trash can shaped like R2-D2
nearly causing a pile-up in a highway game of finders keepers.

At Exit 11A to Fayetteville, a neon
yellow workout shirt,
followed by a dark jacket,
then the dump:
a book with the cover blown open,
two boxes,
and a wad of trash bags
heaped on the curve
and heading south.

Tributary

You make God a woman,
tell elephant jokes,
spill small-talk words
hoping a few I like
will sift out.
But love is better felt
in deluges than trickles.
You considered writing a letter,
carving runnels of words
into the landscape
between our houses.
But paper obliges dams
where love, as all forces of impulse,
forges torrents,
runs away from roads,
chisels rivers that flow off-map.

You Tell Me The Constellations

You tell me the constellations,
place light at its beginning,
bring us into science,
bring reason to my body.
I imagine then I am quiet,
satisfied you have counted me
beyond addition and into fact.

But this is another
something I pretend,
like a bone house
or a strategy of maps.
It is my misimagination
to leave out your real life.

It makes poetry plain
to say I miss you.
I rest like rocks in your garden,
brought home from the ocean,
and practice short memory.
I wear expectation long in the sleeve,
believe you when you tell me
there are more galaxies
and more still,
and names for every one of them.

We Talk This Way Now

Now we talk about safety, quiet,
the possibility of wasted time.
Stringing words, taking aspirin,
lipstick accumulated on the rim of a coffee cup.
All that the razor missed, your face in certain light.
The people who don't know where I am right now.
Humidity that does not stick. Rain falling in sunlight,
green shirts, my hair collected in the wrinkles.
The way words hang on buttons.
How you look back when you close the door, sometimes,
wait for the air seeping through the jamb.

the way they always call her honey

Say there is a woman
of a certain age, some education,
thoughtfulness rampant and aplenty
Say she is a lot like me
Let's say, she is you

She is in love, overworked,
leafs through her papers,
misses something

Lists, some of them important,
crumple into a cushion
for lost things in the bottom
of her bag

She partakes of worry and
the drinking girl's diet,
wears the shoes,
eats because she knows she can,
waits rather than seeks

At a red light late in the day
inertia pulls hard
on her limbs

It's not so much love
as a love story
she tells

Buying groceries she runs into
her first Sunday School teacher
Makes her want to cry
the way teacher
calls her honey

doing Ophelia's mad scene

Surrender grows little legs
and you sink into
the summer of casual disasters.
All the meanings of grief wear you.
You are stretched, restless, overfed.

You tumble without promise,
and the smallest of you goes under watch:
the line by your lips,
your silence at the high tides,
your want to drift.
Even the movement of your hands
leaves nothing about you simple.

All math and maps abandon you.
You slip in calculation and direction.
You state good night for good day.
You blink, so deep is the bruise.
You forget where or what to be.

Offstage your dilemma goes unmarked,
so that your skin begins
to evaporate.
Breathless, drowned, sad girl
driven up the tree:
Hamlet's mad desire always
ranked before your own.

You are casting all the while
friable bits of you wash
off-and-gone in water
below the branches.

Feral Love

When curiosity strikes you as it never has before and you leave your car in the Gas Mart parking lot so you can go over and talk to him, he's going to tell you that God told him to do this, and you won't be the least bit surprised.

That's pretty much what you expect him to say.

Why else would he be standing where you exit onto Robinson from Northwest 4th, wearing his Dale Jr. hat with grease stains on the bill just where the tips of his right index, middle and ring fingers would land.

And with the sign, of course.

The sign, a sheet of plywood cut in half and spray painted white, I LOVE MY WIFE in tall black letters. Something about the sign scares you a little. You wonder why no one else has stopped to ask. The cops, he says, when he was over on Reno. Made him move. His own safety, though just how safe either of you are inches from downtown Wednesday lunch traffic coating you in dust and the relic ashes of thousands of cigarette butts is a question you'd debate. You find out only so much: that he is sixteen days from the second anniversary and feels ashamed.

It's instinct, really, when someone ends a sentence with *ashamed* to say *of what*.

He shrugs. When traffic is slowed by the light change a man riding shotgun in a Kia looks over a while, gives a thumbs up. I don't want her to regret me, the sign man adds, flashing the shy thumbs-up in return.

Man of few words to be holding such a big sign.

You want to say to him you know what he means. That has to be why you linger so long in that deserted lot, just as many people driving by watching you as watching him, Sonic wrapper blown against your leg, traffic lights swinging in electromagnetic hum. But then you just clap the guy on the back and walk away.

Now That We Know the Route We Are Taking

Now That We Know the Route We Are Taking

We were wondering how it might go again,
and this is it: another one of those talks
that happen on the edge of a holiday.
We are passing in and or out and or through
of a quick trip home and catch up
like branches in a frozen pond,
like a verse of a song four decades old
where someone's singing *man,*
it's been too long.

We end up standing
the way you always stand
in small towns, near the highway,
and we're wondering if we've got a minute.
Tires chorus behind us, wash us in dust,
and we hover like ones on a mission
interrupted. We weigh out facts enough
to fit our minute, spill them into conversation,
punctuate said facts with *yeah,*
is that right,
smile.

A year.
We're thinking it's been a year,
but in that way a year
is more like three or four.
That last time we lurked in the doorway
of the catfish place, impediments
to the people ebbing through and out and in,
mostly ones we did not know anymore,
or knew just enough to shout
How y'all doing.
But not really asking.

We're reminded
of news we already know:
how Coach, who was old back when
we were kids, retired; and how Cassie's dad
has passed. Add in that now our own dads
have passed and we're both sorry
and should have mentioned it before,
but we both get it
and it's okay.

Had we bothered to plan this,
had we thought ahead to probabilities
or even sureties, we might
have planned a better where,
instead of one parking lot over
from where the Dairy Queen finally died.
We're unsure if this is meant to be historic.
And besides, it's alright sometimes
for there not to be any pictures.

We're nearly done talking,
the wind scraping away
whole swaths of conversation,
so we neither of us know
if these are reminiscences,
or just goodbyes.
Cue *Auld Lang Syne*.
In our own cars, we wave,
turn onto the highway
as if we're heading the same direction,
absently tune for a radio station
playing something to fit the moment,
saying how long it's been.

House Dreams

We drive up a lane,
all cottages and stone walls,
thinking we need something with character.
Exuberant yards front the houses
and rest ameba-like boundaries
so haphazardly against the road
we aren't sure where to park.
She's got to sell, getting divorced,
she tells us straightaway,
a fact we'd have guessed,
as she begins our tour halting and weepy.
First we see the lot between house and barn,
where suddenly there's a girl, very nearly a ghost,
with spun hair and age indeterminate.
Two small cats trail after,
springing through the green.
My daughter, the woman gestures
to the disappearing girl
as one trying to catch a feather,
tells us the girl's all ready to go.

She takes us through the whole grounds,
left unprepared for company.
We skip over someone's grandfather's tools,
sidestep a maze of collapsing gopher holes.
We smell the wild sweet onions,
crush the new spring grass.
The woman, now with a tissue
dabbing her face,
points to the blackberry vines
and the wild grapes,
then where downspouts are new,
the eaves repaired.
Soon we're inside where large
arched doorways yawn
into tiny rooms swelling
with antique furniture.

We smell lemons, furniture
polish, and old quilts.
The tour takes in the screened
porch facing west,
the laundry floor
where the old well used to be.
She forgets how the septic works,
says possibly she can call her husband,
if we really really want to know.

The woman cries and smiles,
or maybe she smiles then cries,
so hard for us to tell.
She indicates all the places
in this house love could go,
ends with her hand lighting
on a pile of books,
The Child's Guide to Divorce,
unopened, on top.
Furniture? Yes, if we want
any furniture, just offer and ask.
All quality stuff,
and everything must go.
She laughs at the awkwardness
of her own sales pitch.

We thank her, thank her
on the way to the car,
thank her still more,
breathe into the escape
closed car doors bring.
She tos-and-fros
from yard to road
as we begin to back away,
signals us to roll a window down.
We're to call with whatever
questions we might have.
Any time is fine.

She hardly ever sleeps,
and she just knows
she'll see us again.

Quiet, Like Snow Had Fallen

On the first of March,
after its birth announcement
had been sung from the hilltops,
the storm chose not to come, after all.
Half an inch of dry, soft ice
pelleted the scraggly grass,
which, for this being the spit-out end
of the Ozarks, ain't much.

I drove eleven hours yesterday,
from south Texas to here,
only for a season to die mid-journey.
I went absent decent radio stations,
over and around Austin chaos,
in and out of homebound semis,
fighting loose rental car steering,
dreading work awaiting me,
only to land home weak
and road-blind.

But today I woke up to quiet,
like snow had fallen. Vertigo presses
the backs of my eyes.
The weatherman has issued
an apology and thanks the internet
for caring. It has gotten
so the weather can not change its mind,
so driving can not relieve the exhaustion
brought down from winter skies.
It is as if we have surrendered
both lingering and anticipation.

Considering What is Known of Charley

In college Charley boxed
Gold Gloves for a pint:
half before the fight, half after.
It was a gain purely earned,
a simple conceiving of risk and reward.
Work, as it'd be known
in the traditional sense,
another matter altogether.
It was never enough
not to think too much, but at least
he could say when.
From behind half-moon glasses
he studied parts he'd exhumed
from a long-dead radio and laid
out on the oiled wood table.
He paced himself: glasses off, back on.
When he'd reasoned out the roles
of every part, how each locked
into another, he assembled them
with speed otherwise incalculable
in handwork. From the hammock
in his mother's yard, he abated the dim
afternoons, music drifting
out from the house, at peace
with the science of figuring.

He Steals Blue Cars

He steals blue cars
though not just blue
but teal
cobalt
and azure

Metallic
Bondo-ed
chalky
rusted

He got him one
of those Le Sabres once

Floated downtown
in a land barge
life sweet
behind the wheel

Ways I Am Like a Tumbleweed

prickly
for starters

dry sense of humor
though not as dry as it seems from a distance

get lost
on open highways in the spring

always leave things
behind when I travel

watch trains longingly
but never board

bolt
if crowded

may/may not be of Russian extraction
depending who you ask

winter
really does me in

trouble getting over
barbed wire fences

cows
think they'll like me

then
they don't

The Suburbanite's Non-Guide to Lawn Care:
Subtitle *The Death of a Dream*:
Loma Linda, Missouri c. 2016

The first year in a new house
is when you speak your wishes.
So I said:
gardens.
A big open lawn
and room for gardens.
But suburban lawns
are the wishes of the naïve.

We buy a place
with a few established gardens,
but established by what means?
Mold rot wafts out from the roadside beds,
a spreading sickly purple,
and so they have to go.
Yuccas emerge among the tulips,
followed by sunflowers in
a hideous floral mélange,
and so they go.
Live hollies,
packed inch by inch
with black widows,
and so in Year One,
they all go.

I buy twenty colorful flower pots,
plant flowers in every color.
Admire the fruits of my green thumb
from my picture window.

Year Two,
and enough already
of the mosquitos breeding Zika
and baby moles drowning

in the fountain out back,
so the fountain goes.
I unearth an iris graveyard
and an undiggable
layer of chert.
The spearmint percolating
along the fence mutates
into an unkillable weed,
declines my invitation to go.
I am up at 6:30 on Sunday,
ahead of the humidity,
pulling stickers
and crabgrass clusters
when my husband yells:
We have a beautiful yard.
Why are you always working on it?
Why don't you just enjoy it?

The perennials in colorful pots
failed the winter.
I buy more,
replant.
Add in zucchini,
yellow squash,
tomatoes and jalapenos.
Raccoons execute a home invasion
in the dark of night,
abscond with everything
but the seedy
sun-blackened peppers.

Year Three:
we've lost the interest
of the guys who do our mowing.
Differences in artistic visions
bring about the unintentional demise
of the uncultivated prairie garden
look for which I was going.

Now the guys come later,
and less often,
ask for beer.
The caddy-corner neighbor
turns his riding mower
around in the street,
accidentally
takes out five feet's worth
of our grass.
Hint, hint.

The flower pots have diminished
in number and condition,
for reasons I can not determine.
But I give this
flowers in pots thing another go.

Years Four and/or Five:
a strange tall grass I've never seen before
comes up with the lilies,
winds between their stalks
so that I can't pull one without
killing both.
We buy a new bird bath
to reside near the driveway.
But to our birds it's more curiosity than home.
It's always muddy,
and something that might be a snake
keeps leaving trails
in the grit of the bowl.
Prairie roses extend tendrils,
look around,
and die away confused.
My attempt at adding Missouri
wildflowers to the yard
is mistaken by the mowers as
botanical mutiny
and mercifully Weed-Eated away.

I neither find the old
flowerpots
nor buy any new.

Present Day:
we've let our grass die.
Again.
Wide swaths
in every shade of brown
crisp up across the front half-acre.
Johnson grass
so tall it gives off shade
sways in every flower bed.
The man in the mansion across the street
hates us,
or so I'm guessing.
He of the lawn tractor, irrigation system,
Brush Hog for which he
has no purpose.
Has his lawn care guys on speed dial.
Every spring they paint his
grass green,
smoke in the road
while they watch each remote-controlled
sprinkler head emerge.

And every summer
they fight blight,
termites, red ants,
wild elms and blackberries,
thorny dandelions.
And every night
McMansion Man pours
thousands of gallons of water
onto to his globally warming territory,
so every two or three days,
even in deadliest of heat,
he can mow.

His yard and ours,
testaments to the dreamers
and the doers,
I think,
and watch the grass die
from behind my picture windows.

one a snow dog, one not

We talked of the coming snow day,
the groceries to get,
the food to make,
whether work would be open
and school closed.
But we did not tell the dogs:
one a snow dog, one not,
so the seven inches of crystalized
water surprised them both,
released a flurry of reactions.
One dog, who dislikes the cold
and hates being wet,
accused the stuff of frigid evil,
of dampening her air and earth,
so after failing to drive it off
with the fury of her barking
she returned to the warm and dry.
But the other, the snow dog,
struck still in wonder.
She plunged her face
into a bank,
inhaled and exhaled,
ate a few bites—
first big and fast, then
slow and savoring—
like one too long denied cake.
Snow dog, old and arthritic,
sprang out one, two, three hops,
looked back at the divots
her paws had made.
From there she ambled,
paused then ambled,
paused,
eyes closed,
face turned upward,
welcomed winter to gather
over her dark coat.

Jesus Calls from Tampa

Jesus calls from Tampa,
having landed at the Super 8,
having ridden his decrepit pick-up too far,
having one highway patrolman convinced of his pilgrimage.
He wants to know: did you find the letter?

Eight pages of explanation,
of poetry and doctrine, the spelling out
of how we can all be saved.
He's got the words and the love, the truth and the time.
He wants to know: do you believe him?

Your name is Chris,
you say. You live in Missouri.
You used to work at the chicken place.
Your social worker is looking for you.
Do you know they're worried?

But Jesus is discovering,
is finding lyrics out there,
is hearing melodies on the highways,
is seeing clear to the end, is seeing it's not so bad,
not nearly what we thought at all.
He wants to know: do you see it too?

you'll hate her for this, but it's true

you'll hate her for this, but it's true:
she loves that she was beautiful.
She craves a space where she can mourn it,
but good luck finding someone
patient enough to give you that.
She's tired, but trying the grown-up thing.
She wants to be called baby
down in her pink-washed baby heart,
but no one came to meet her there.
So now she's saying please and thank you.
Yeah, we're doing that grown-up thing.
She's barely longing, and just for certain small pieces:
like boys and butterflies and hearts
because that is all girls take from poems.
She did, anyway, once upon a time.
All things pretty began at girl,
all worth having is from way back when.
She stopped drinking wine from plastic cups,
gave up wonder for a landscaped life.
But she is such a beautiful idea.
She tells love stories to herself.

Flock

They alight late,
swoop up wrapped
in scarves and shawls
all wrong
for hot September
breezes. They cheep
as they flitter
through the door,
just loud enough
for us to notice,
but not enough
for us to hear.

They observe us,
observing them,
then turn
in formation,
glide to the front
of the room,
assume a graceful
collective perch.
They've come,
they sing out,
to tell us about art.

Not art.

ART.

What art is.
What it can be.
How one can be changed by it.

They hang
their words around us,
watch us
for sudden moves.

90

Unseen bracelets
clank
and jingle.
Fringe and bell sleeves
waft down
like purple feathers.

I lose the thread
of their song,
mesmerized by their variations
on 1981's Stevie Nicks,
watch them wing
along the tailwinds
of their trilling
polyphonous anthem.

Us and Chihuly's Tree

We shuffle the paved path
through the curated forest thick
with flying bugs and humidity.
Not so many tourists as to overwhelm,
enough to generate a hum equal
that of the cicadas clustered
in leaves overhead.
Every drop of air sticks to me,
while I am bumped by a squad
of elementary schoolers
counting blue things.

We have come to see the Chihuly
scattered, mounted,
among the oaks and short-leaf pines.
Artfully, of course. Organic,
organic. Everyone milling
along says the word,
whispers the word.
Should we focus on the color
or the juxtaposition.
Nature tones,
then the jewel tones.
Glass spikes in grass.
Balls clustered in murky water.
Squigglies in a rowboat,
dry and run aground.
Organic, organic,
it is all so damned organic.

A woman with a German accent
and no boundaries for approaching strangers
pulls my phone from my hand.
I take for you, she says.
Smiles with tall teeth,
her hair effortlessly cool.

We cuddle up.
I clutch my latte cup at my side,
twist to an angle apropos the art.
The stream of onlookers recedes,
gives us our moment
to capture the frame: just us
and Chihuly's tree in static explosion.
Its crown, a waning ameba.
Its limbs, intense as pathogen.
Your face, all bemusement.
Something with wings beating fast.
And, god, the sweat.

A wine truck sits
at the end of the path
making slushies of white
zinfandel and pink lemonade,
four dollars. The line is long.
We wait, debate not waiting.
Voices burble over the canopy,
wend around tree trunks.
Out of our sight, someone
—without a "You have to"—calls
"See this! See this!"

The Fate of Some Minnows: Comanche Lake c. 1977

We went into the minnow room,
the slender sliver of porch
slapped-up and screened-in
alongside the bait shop,
to observe the minnows in their
unnatural habitat:
an RC Cola cooler box,
lids removed,
that once sold cold drinks,
probably in the shop next door.

The whirring box sat on the screened wall
so it caught the sun in the early part of the day.
They swam by the hundreds, maybe more,
tiny schools in a tinier ocean.
The water rippled almost imperceptibly, clear,
though green lake scum grew thick globs
ending in fine hair
all along the sides.

From time to time we watched
a man from the shop, cooked tan,
come in to fill tubs once used for the likes
of Blue Bonnet margarine
with the borrowed lake water.
He eyeballed the haul of each,
took a small net like the ones used
for gold fish from a nail,
and chased up a scoop or two of fleeing minnows.

I knew the fate of these plugged-in fish,
but I must not have thought about it.
I remember nothing else that I know
to have happened:
my Dad buying boxes of damp dirt
filled with worms,

his fishing,
or his even liking to fish;

only that if you touched the surface of the
cooler water with your finger tip
softly enough
the minnows still darted away,
but returned quick and curious;
and I knew that if you moved slowly enough
you could lower your finger,
then maybe all your fingers,
into the water without the minnows
leaving again;
that just like minnows
on the lake shoreline did
when you stepped slowly enough,
these minnows lingered with you
in the shallow water,
glancing against your skin.

Weeknight Revival: Countryside Baptist Church
c. 1975

Lightning bugs, starlight,
lawn chairs littering wide open space:
practiced in parades and watermelon festivals
and seasons that bore their markers,
I expected a potluck picnic,
a bit of dancing down by the creek.
Maybe a finale
replete with sparklers.
But where she took me
was just a church.

Granny's church. After cutting me,
lone calf, from the family herd —
my parents not the churchy types,
summer idylls a lure to my siblings.
Granny called it the new church,
a tornado having taken the old one (and her
handmade seat cushion she kept
permanently on her pew)
some fifteen or twenty years before;
a plain box of building aside a curving highway,
the end point of which I had never met,
the arc of it almost always empty.
I had seen revival tents in fields,
Christmas lights dangled from canopies,
microphones for singers and bands,
but my mother had said those
were just good places
to get chiggers.

The service was the same:
the same people I saw on the Sundays we came
with our neighbors, the same dour songs,
the same offering envelopes with their pockets
for paper money, tabs for coins. I had found them

folded into boats and planes before, and once
someone left one on the seat
puffed up like a paper balloon.
I pulled them one after another from the
stack tucked in the hymnal racks,
attempted to craft art of my boredom,
my handiwork collecting
crumpled on the floor.

As for what drew the congregation,
I kept my attention attuned just enough
that I can pull forth only this:
the back of my granny's head,
her curly hair flattened and mussed,
as she stood to sing;
the preacher's crescendoing
into just-about-the-end,
accompanied by the clang of the overly loud piano
played by someone with no sense of grace.
He called to the lost:
come down front,
and a handful of them did.
They wobbled, eyes closed,
lifted their arms as if to make Vs or Ws.
The preacher laid his hand on their shoulders.
One man cried, they all said thank you,
and then everybody left.

Driving back into town,
the railroad crossing signals lit up
just as we mounted the tracks.
The sign was on for Harold's bar.
A blue glow emitted from the wall
of dressing rooms in Hicks' department store.
Our passing under streetlights Dopplered
off the windows of downtown,
and I wondered
lost from what.

and they continue to pray for Evelin's salvation

Hiatt watches morning moons hanging in new daylight.
They mark imperial cardinals, slow and faded in the haze.
They shoo out old dogs to stand guard on back porches,
and they continue to pray for Evelin's salvation.

Hiatt busily forges platters of bacon and eggs.
They drop unwrapped biscuits onto microwavable plates.
They open tin foil trays of sticky cherry danish,
and they continue to pray for Evelin's salvation.

Hiatt sends the willing into war and into work.
They hold Arma game day sacred, keep it safe from crime.
They'll show shiny and early for church come next Sunday,
and they continue to pray for Evelin's salvation.

Hiatt men sit on benches one corner over from the bank.
They think no one gets the weather talk of nothing else.
They've lost even the memories of things they used to say,
and they continue to pray for Evelin's salvation.

Hiatt women eat their agonies, wear their weariness and grief.
They can't enjoy life when they're feeling too much love.
They want an end to wanting, and what they stand for to stay,
and they continue to pray for Evelin's salvation.

Hiatt leaves mostly-finished Crown Royals under the bridge.
They're pulled by fast food and Wal-Mart ten miles away.
They feel the curled-up edges of place as much as anybody can,
and they continue to pray for Evelin's salvation.

Hiatt fetes young ones leaving with homemade jams and quilts.
They pack their cars with spells to bring them all back home.
They still hope for hope chests and daughters moved away,
and they continue to pray for Evelin's salvation.

Hiatt sits split four-square, quiet as a picture.
They do not meet momentum when it comes jetlagged and dark.
They've put celebrations of its arrival on indefinite hold,
and they continue to pray for Evelin's salvation.

Summer: Gardens: Back When

Summer: Oklahoma: mid-1970s

My grandparents call:
we are to come pick
the tomatoes and the squash—
the yellow and the zucchini.
Mostly my mother does the labor,
collects bounty in paper grocery bags
until they grow heavy enough to tear.
I wind among resplendent green stalks,
feel their prickles sting my hand:
corn and okra yet to come.
The smell of garden dirt
draws me close.

Summer: My parents' house: late 1970s

My grandfather's icebox tomatoes
have a good year.
Several rest in Corning Ware
balanced around our kitchen.
Too many for us, my mother says,
makes homemade salad dressing
in the tomatoes' honor.
I eat them, gorge on them,
drink the dressing mixed with seeds
from the cold saucer,
discover a forever love.
Acid burns leave raw the skin
around my mouth.

Summer: The street in front of our house: early 1980s

A woman from my mother's homemakers' club,
and later a man my dad
kind of knows from work,
pull their cars up

where I shoot basketball in the driveway.
Each presents me sacks of produce,
tell me their gardens made too much;
tell my confused face
Just give 'em to your mama,
or something like that.
My mother comes to the door
as the man's long car slides away,
hollers how much she loves plums.
Well, just the six trees, he says, and waves.
The crumpled bag swallows
her face as she sucks up
the luscious scent of fruit.

Summer: Our kitchen on 5th Street: mid-1980s

My mother is making green apple jelly.
She's taken them all,
including the bird-pecked,
even those bruised and rotting
on the ground. Flavor, she says, holding
up the brown spots to me.
She names people to give jars,
sends a few with my father
each time he goes out to visit.
Her last garden was all gladiolas.
Paraffin and canning gear
overwhelm the kitchen.
This may be the last batch
of jelly she makes.

Summer: The lot by Frances's mother's house:
I don't remember when

But I don't remember my mother
gardening after then.
Not vegetables, anyway.
Not in the heat and the weeds.
Not pinching potato bugs to death.

She and a couple of friends
put in a group effort,
garden hauls needing to be shared.
It's my mother's week to water
and to collect what she wants.
We take a cardboard box
my dad fished from the pharmacy trash,
a film of magazine pages
lining the bottom.
We layer in a few of this,
a couple of that,
but none of the other.
She's saying she and Dad don't need much.
She'll bag up some of her take
to feed other people,
sets tomatoes for me
delicately
in one corner.

About the Author

Joey Brown is the author of two poetry collections: *The Feral Love Poems* (Hungry Buzzard Press) and *Oklahomaography* (Mongrel Empire Press). Her poems and prose have appeared in a number of literary journals including *The Red Earth Review, Concho River Review, The Langdon Review of the Arts in Texas, Tulsa Review, Oklahoma Review, The San Pedro River Review*, and others. She frequently performs her poetry at festivals and conferences around Texas, Oklahoma, New Mexico, Kansas, and Missouri. Joey holds an M.A. in Creative Writing and a Ph.D. in Interdisciplinary Studies from the University of Oklahoma. She lives with her husband, novelist Michael Howarth, and their pack of congenial rescue dogs on the western edge of the Missouri Ozarks.